FREE Test Taking Tips Video/DVD Offer

To better serve you, we created videos covering test taking tips that we want to give you for FREE. **These videos cover world-class tips that will help you succeed on your test.**

We just ask that you send us feedback about this product. Please let us know what you thought about it—whether good, bad, or indifferent.

To get your **FREE videos**, you can use the QR code below or email freevideos@studyguideteam.com with "Free Videos" in the subject line and the following information in the body of the email:

     a. The title of your product

     b. Your product rating on a scale of 1-5, with 5 being the highest

     c. Your feedback about the product

If you have any questions or concerns, please don't hesitate to contact us at info@studyguideteam.com.

Thank you!

CogAT Grade 4 Level 10 Workbook
Gifted and Talented Test Preparation with CogAT Practice Questions for Forms 7 and 8

Joshua Rueda

Interested in buying more than 10 copies of our product? Contact us about bulk discounts:
bulkorders@studyguideteam.com

ISBN 13: 9781637758151
ISBN 10: 1637758154

Table of Contents

Welcome

Dear Reader,

Welcome to your new Test Prep Books study guide! We are pleased that you chose us to help you prepare for your exam. There are many study options to choose from, and we appreciate you choosing us. Studying can be a daunting task, but we have designed a smart, effective study guide to help prepare you for what lies ahead.

Whether you're a parent helping your child learn and grow, a high school student working hard to get into your dream college, or a nursing student studying for a complex exam, we want to help give you the tools you need to succeed. We hope this study guide gives you the skills and the confidence to thrive, and we can't thank you enough for allowing us to be part of your journey.

In an effort to continue to improve our products, we welcome feedback from our customers. We look forward to hearing from you. Suggestions, success stories, and criticisms can all be communicated by emailing us at info@studyguideteam.com.

Sincerely,
Test Prep Books Team

FREE Videos/DVD OFFER

Doing well on your exam requires both knowing the test content and understanding how to use that knowledge to do well on the test. We offer completely FREE test taking tip videos. **These videos cover world-class tips that you can use to succeed on your test.**

To get your **FREE videos**, you can use the QR code below or email freevideos@studyguideteam.com with "Free Videos" in the subject line and the following information in the body of the email:

 a. The title of your product
 b. Your product rating on a scale of 1-5, with 5 being the highest
 c. Your feedback about the product

If you have any questions or concerns, please don't hesitate to contact us at info@studyguideteam.com.

1

Quick Overview

As your child or student draws closer to taking their exam, being prepared becomes more and more important. Thankfully, they have this study guide to help them get ready. Use this guide to help keep their studying on track and refer to it often.

This study guide contains several key sections that will help your child be successful on their exam. The guide has tips for what they should do the night before and the day of the test. Also included are test-taking tips. These tips will help equip them to read, assess, and answer test questions.

A large part of the guide is devoted to showing your child what content to expect on the exam and to helping them better understand that content. We also show them practice test questions so that they can see how well they understand the concept of the exam. Then, answer explanations are provided so that they can understand why they missed certain questions.

Your child shouldn't try to cram the night before their exam. First, their retention of the information will be low. Their time would be better used by reviewing information they already know rather than trying to learn a lot of new information. Second, they will likely become stressed as they try to gain a large amount of knowledge in a short amount of time. Third, they will be deprived of sleep. So be sure that your child goes to bed at a reasonable time the night before. Being well-rested helps them focus and remain calm.

Be sure that your child eats a substantial breakfast the morning of the exam. If they are taking the exam in the afternoon, be sure that they have a good lunch as well. Being hungry is distracting and can make it difficult to focus. They have hopefully spent lots of time preparing for the exam. Don't let an empty stomach get in the way of success!

Encourage your child to pace themself during the exam. They shouldn't rush. Your child should use all of the allotted time if needed.

Tell your child that it's important to remain positive while taking the exam even if they feel like they are performing poorly. Thinking about the content they should have mastered will not help them perform better on the exam.

Once the exam is complete, allow your child to take some time to relax. Even if they feel that they need to study for other things, they will be well served by some down time before they begin studying again. It's often easier to convince a child to study if they know that it will come with a reward!

2

Test Taking Strategies

1. Predicting the Answer

When your child feels confident in their preparation for a multiple-choice test, they should try predicting the answer before looking at the answer choices. By predicting the answer before viewing the choices, they will less likely be distracted by an incorrect answer choice. They will feel more confident in their selection if they evaluate the question, predict the answer, and then find their prediction among the answer choices. After using this strategy, they should be sure to go through all of the answer choices carefully and completely. If your child feels unprepared, they should not attempt to predict the answers. This would be a waste of time and an opportunity for their mind to wander in the wrong direction.

2. Examine the Whole Question

Too often, test takers scan a multiple-choice question and immediately jump to the answer choices. Test authors are aware of this common impatience, and they will sometimes prey upon it. A test author will include answer choices that would seem correct if the question isn't fully understood. The only way to avoid falling into this trap is to examine the whole question carefully before looking at the answer choices. The CogAT and NNAT exams specifically focus on the ability of the test taker to analyze the relationship between all of the components of a question in order to find the correct answer. Therefore, it is crucial that you encourage your child to study an entire question before moving on to the answer choices.

3. Looking for Wrong Answers

One way to simplify a multiple-choice question is to eliminate all of the answer choices that are clearly wrong. There will usually be at least one choice that can be dismissed right away. Once the obviously incorrect answers have been eliminated, the remaining choices may be considered.

4. Don't Overanalyze

When individuals are nervous, their brains will often run wild, causing them to make associations and discover clues that don't exist. If you feel that this may be a problem for your child, remind them that they should do whatever they can to slow down during the test. They can try taking a deep breath or counting to ten. They should also be sure to not overthink the question. The associations that are shown in the question should lead your child to figure out the answer, so they need to be sure that the associations or clues that they are using when looking for an answer are derived from the question and not from their imagination.

5. No Need for Panic

It is wise to learn as many strategies as possible before taking a multiple-choice test, but it is likely that your child will come across a few questions for which they don't know the answer. In this situation, they should avoid panicking. Getting one incorrect answer does not mean failure. When they find a question

3

that they either don't understand or don't know how to answer, they should take a deep breath and just do their best. Encourage your child to look over the entire question slowly and carefully. Then, they should read all of the answer choices carefully. After eliminating obviously wrong answers, they can make a selection and move on to the next question.

6. First Instinct

Many people struggle with multiple-choice tests because they overthink the questions. If your child has studied for their test and understands the format of the test, they should be prepared to trust their first instinct once they have evaluated the question and the answer choices. There is a great deal of research suggesting that the mind can come to the correct conclusion quickly once it has obtained all of the relevant information. At times, it may seem as if one's intuition is working faster than one's reasoning mind. This may in fact be true. The student should verify their instinct by working out the reasons that it should be trusted.

7. Reading Every Answer Choice

It may seem obvious, but your child should always look at every one of the answer choices! Too many test takers fall into the habit of scanning the question and assuming that they understand the question. From there, they pick the first answer choice that seems correct. Test takers who look over and analyze all of the answer choices might discover that one of the latter answer choices is actually *more* correct. Moreover, looking at all of the answer choices might remind the student of an observation they made when looking at the question. This could help them arrive at the correct answer. Sometimes, an incorrect detail in one of the latter answer choices will trigger their memory and enable them to find the right answer. Failing to consider all of the answer choices is like not reading all of the items on a restaurant menu: your child might miss out on the perfect choice.

8. Rephrasing to Understand

Sometimes, a question on a multiple-choice test is difficult not because of what it asks but because of how it is written. If this is the case, the question or answer choices can be viewed in different ways, such as looking at the question from right to left rather than only from left to right. This process serves a couple of important purposes. First, it forces the student to concentrate on the core of the question so that they can understand it well. Mentally "rephrasing" the question by viewing and analyzing the patterns in a different order will concentrate their mind on the key patterns and relationships in the question. Second, it will present the information to their mind in a fresh way. This process may trigger them to discover a connection that they didn't observe before.

9. No Patterns

Answer choices will never be chosen based on patterns. The questions are scrambled and delivered in a random order. Any attempt to discern a pattern in the answer choices is a waste of time and a distraction from the real work of taking the test.

4

Introduction

Function and Administration

The Cognitive Abilities Test (CogAT) is a test used for entrance or placement decisions into gifted and talented programs and classes across the United States. The exam offers K–12 assessment in the areas of reasoning and problem-solving abilities through Verbal, Nonverbal, and Quantitative batteries.

Administration of the CogAT depends on the school district offering the test. Reach out to your school district to see when they offer the test and how to register for it. Retesting is also dependent on the school offering the exam. Many school districts do not offer the CogAT again in a single academic year once the student has taken the exam, but this may vary in different areas.

Test Format

The CogAT exam Grade 4 Level 10 is made up of 3 batteries: Verbal, Nonverbal, and Quantitative. Level 10 is for fourth grade students who are at the age of 10 years old. The Level 10 CogAT has 176 questions. Within the three batteries of Verbal, Nonverbal, and Quantitative are the following subsections:

- Verbal
    - Verbal Classification
    - Verbal Analogies
    - Sentence Completion
- Quantitative
    - Number Series
    - Number Puzzles
    - Number Analogies
- Nonverbal
    - Figure Matrices
    - Paper Folding
    - Figure Classification

Scoring

Students do not lose points for guessing incorrectly, so they should always mark an answer on the CogAT exam even if they are not sure it's correct. There are several different ways to look at scores in the CogAT exam. The raw score shows the number of answers guessed correctly out of the number of questions. The Universal Scale Score (USS) is the three scores for the batteries, and then that is converted into one Composite score. The Standard Age Score (SAS) has a maximum score of 160 and shows the potential and rate of development of that student. The Percentile Rank (PR) is used to compare the student to others in their age and grade. Finally, the Stanine (S) score is simplified on a scale from 1 to 9 and normalized for ages and grades.

Recent/Future Developments

The latest version of the CogAT is the CogAT Form 7, which was developed with non-native English speakers in mind.

As you study for your test, we'd like to take the opportunity to remind you that you are capable of great things! With the right tools and dedication, you truly can do anything you set your mind to. The fact that you are holding this book right now shows how committed you are. In case no one has told you lately, you've got this! Our intention behind including this coloring page is to give you the chance to take some time to engage your creative side when you need a little brain-break from studying. As a company, we want to encourage people like you to achieve their dreams by providing good quality study materials for the tests and certifications that improve careers and change lives. As individuals, many of us have taken such tests in our careers, and we know how challenging this process can be. While we can't come alongside you and cheer you on personally, we can offer you the space to recall your purpose, reconnect with your passion, and refresh your brain through an artistic practice. We wish you every success, and happy studying!

Verbal

Verbal Classification

Description
In the Verbal Classification section of the Level 10 CogAT test, the student's ability to read and recognize similarities will be tested. These questions give three words that are in some way alike or related. Students must recognize the similarity and pick the answer choice that maintains the same relationship. For example, a set of words might name *red, blue,* and *orange*. The student must choose the answer that falls into the same category, which would be any other color such as *purple, green, yellow,* etc. These questions differ from previous levels because students are given words instead of pictures at this stage.

Relevance
Students are required not only to read the words but also to comprehend what they mean and relate them to the others. Such concepts apply to associations that students need to make in their everyday lives. For example, they should be able to evaluate the weather and determine what clothes to wear that are appropriate for the current conditions. Cold weather should be associated with a jacket and gloves. If the weather is warm, students should recognize that they will not need a hat and gloves; rather, they may need to wear lighter clothes to be comfortable.

Tips for Parents
Parents can help students prepare for this section by practicing association skills. Write down some categories, make a list of words that relate to each category, and present them to the student. One possible category could be *shapes*, and the list of related words could include *circle, triangle,* and *square*. Give this list to the student and ask for a fourth word that would relate in the same way. Possible answers include *rectangle, oval,* or *pentagon*.

It may also be helpful to discuss with the student the relationship between the words. After identifying the relation, the student may come up with even more words that would also fit into the group. To provide a deeper understanding, the parent could ask the student to come up with a set of words and present them to the parent. Once the parent gives an answer, they can discuss the relation that they each see in the words. Any type of argument or discussion to prove an answer correct is helpful in obtaining a deeper knowledge of the subject.

Sample Problem
The following problem is a sample of what students might see in the Verbal Classification section of the test.

> # car, van, jeep
> _____
> a) truck b) door c) window d) lights

Explanation of Sample Problem

These words are related in that they are all types of vehicles. The correct answer must be another type of vehicle, so it is Choice *A*: truck. The other answers are parts on a vehicle. While they are related to vehicles, they do not name types of vehicles, so they do not qualify as answers.

Verbal Analogies

Description

The Verbal Analogies section of the Level 10 CogAT test assesses the student's ability to recognize relationships and apply them. The student will be given one completed analogy followed by one that needs to be completed. Once the student determines how the first two words are related, they can apply the same relationship to the incomplete analogy and determine the correct answer.

This section is more about individual relationships rather than groups of words. Students may be given the analogy *hunger* : *food* and the word *thirst*. Hunger can be satisfied with food. Applying this concept to *thirst*, the word that completes the analogy should be *drink* because drinks satisfy thirst.

Relevance

These types of relational ideas may prove useful to students as they make decisions. They may see their parents make healthy food choices and recognize the benefits that come as a result. In turn, they may choose to make healthy choices so that they too can reap the benefits.

This can also be helpful in recognizing bad behavior and its consequences. If a student sees another student talk out of turn and lose a privilege, they may decide not to talk out of turn so that they do not lose a privilege. This type of reasoning is very helpful in the growth and development of children.

Tips for Parents

Make sure students know that the first two words are related, and the third word is related to an answer. If students have not encountered analogies before, this format may be confusing at first.

As with the other sections, practicing is also helpful. Parents may give students example analogies and allow students to complete them. They should talk through the relationships and have students make up their own analogy that is related in the same way.

Sample Problem

The following problem is a sample of what students might see in the Verbal Analogies section of the test.

open: close - up:

_____

a) over   c) left
b) down   d) top

Explanation of Sample Problem

The first two words are opposites. The opposite of opening a door is closing it. The third word is *up*, which is the opposite of *down*: Choice *B*. The other choices are related to the third word, but they are not opposites.

Sentence Completion

Description

In the Sentence Completion section of the Level 10 CogAT test, the student's ability to comprehend ideas and complete open-ended questions is tested. Each question in this section consists of a sentence that is missing a word. The student must read and comprehend the sentence before choosing the best word to complete the sentence.

The main point of this section is for students to read and comprehend the topic of each sentence. Once they identify what is happening in the sentence, they can choose the word that best completes each thought. The format will be multiple choice, so students must be able to identify which words make sense in the sentence and which ones do not.

Relevance

Sentence completion may be the most complex of the verbal sections. It encompasses vocabulary, relationships between words, and comprehension of more complex ideas. As students read the sentence, they must define the words in their head and then determine relationships between these words. The relationships can be generalized to form a final idea that explains the entire sentence. Each part of this process teaches students the importance of words and how they are used even in everyday conversation.

Tips for Parents

The best way to prepare your student for this type of problem is encouraging them to read. Reading allows them to develop their comprehension skills and helps them become familiar with more complex words. While reading, students must understand sentences in context, and they must also apply their vocabulary knowledge. The more they read, the more they will develop their overall verbal skills.

Parents may also write sentences that have missing words. They can work with students to review meanings of words and discuss concepts within each sentence. As with the other verbal sections, it may also be helpful to discuss why some words would not fit into a sentence. All of these strategies will help students prepare for the Sentence Completion portion of the test.

Sample Problem

The following problem is a sample of what students might see in the Sentence Completion section of the test.

> **The family was _____ from their long trip and decided to go straight to bed.**
>
> _____
>
> a) hungry   b) energized   c) tired   d) thirsty

Explanation of Sample Problem

The sentence is talking about a family who has just been on a long trip. The end of the sentence explains that they go straight to bed, so the choice of word must relate to this idea. The answer is Choice *C*: tired.

Practice Questions

1.

plate, bowl, spoon

a) dinner   b) cup   c) kitchen

2.

run, skip, jump

a) sit   b) stand   c) walk

3.

win: lose - clean:

a) put away   c) organized
b) neat   d) dirty

4.

dog: puppy - lion:

a) tiger   c) cub
b) cat   d) baby

5.

Sarah had to learn how to _____ before she could go in the pool.

a) swim   b) cook   c) read   d) dive

Answer Explanations

1. B: The given words are kitchen utensils. Out of the answer choices, the only kitchen utensil is *cup*.

2. C: The given words are actions that involve movement. The only answer choice that fits this pattern is *walk*.

3. D: *Win* is the opposite of *lose*, while *clean* is the opposite of *dirty*. The other choices are synonyms of *clean*.

4. C: A baby *dog* is called a *puppy*, and a baby *lion* is called a *cub*.

5. A: Sarah would need to know how to swim before going in the pool. If she didn't know how to swim, going into the pool could be dangerous.

Quantitative

Number Series

Description

In the Number Series section of the Level 10 CogAT test, the student's problem-solving ability will be tested as they reason through a given series of numbers. These numbers will be given in a specific order, and the students will determine the pattern used to find each successive number. Students will then apply this pattern or operation to find the next number in the series.

Possible operations include adding or subtracting the same number each time. Patterns may also include doubling the given number or taking half of it to find the next number in the sequence. There may also be more complex patterns that include adding twice the previous number to find the next number. Each question will have different patterns or operations, but the goal of finding the next number in the series is the same throughout this section.

Relevance

This section is relevant to students because it requires critical thinking skills. They must use their prior knowledge to recognize how the numbers relate to one another. This type of skill is important across all aspects of life as students work to be better problem-solvers. They will use their prior knowledge of sports and build upon it with new knowledge to become better athletes. They will use critical thinking skills to work out problems in their personal life when they have issues with friends instead of just giving up on a friendship. These skills will prove helpful in many aspects of life.

Tips for Parents

It is important that students recognize the objective of each test section. For this section, students will be expected to choose the next number in a series. Parents may start by introducing their child to a given series and asking them what pattern they recognize. If the student struggles at first, parents can offer help in finding the first pattern. They can then explain how to use an operation to find the next number.

It is also important to encourage practice. As students are exposed to more and more series, they will expand their knowledge and develop their problem-solving ability. Parents should come alongside students as they work through these questions, as they may not be accustomed to this type of problem.

Sample Problem

The following problem is a sample of what students might see in the Number Series section of the test.

> ## 2, 4, 8, 16, ___
> _____
> a) 20   b) 24   c) 32   d) 64

14

Explanation of Sample Problem

The answer to the sample problem is *C*. Since the problem gives a series of numbers, the student should recognize that the answer is the next number in the series. Students should recognize that the numbers increase each time, but not by the same amount. To get from one number to the next, the given number is doubled. Using this pattern and applying it to the last number, 16 is doubled to yield 32.

Number Puzzles

Description

In the Number Puzzles section of the Level 10 CogAT test, the student's problem-solving ability will be tested as they determine which answer choice makes a given equation true. The questions in this section will show students an incomplete equation. They will then be expected to choose a number that completes the mathematical sentence. Completing the mathematical sentence includes finding a number that makes a true statement when the operations in the equation are performed.

Examples of number puzzle questions may require students to perform operations in an equation first and then work backwards to find a missing number. For example, in the equation $2 + ? = 4 \times 1$, the missing part is the number being added to the 2 on the left side. By computing 4 times 1, the equation can be simplified to $2 + ? = 4$. Then students will be able to deduce that the missing number is two. To check the work, replace the question mark with 2, which gives the equation $2 + 2 = 4 \times 1$. This equation is a true statement.

Relevance

This section is relevant as students begin to comprehend missing numbers as unknown values and work to find their value. This concept will only grow in higher level math classes when unknown values will be replaced with variables and used to solve for missing quantities or make predictions. The ability of students to recognize and find these missing values will prove helpful for them as they grow as independent thinkers.

Tips for Parents

This section will require students to fill in a missing number in a given equation. The first step is to recognize this type of question. Students should see that there is an equation that is missing a number. The next step is to solve for that missing number. Depending on the equation, this can be done in many ways. The student should simplify the equation as much as possible. Then they should determine what missing number would make the equation a true statement.

This section can be tricky because it may require a knowledge of mathematical properties such as associative, commutative, and distributive. The student should be able to recognize these properties and use them to solve for missing numbers. The best way to become more familiar with and prepared for these questions is to practice finding missing parts of an equation.

Sample Problem

The following problem is a sample of what students might see in the Number Puzzle section of the test.

$$10 - ? = 2 \times 3$$

a) 3   b) 4   c) 6   d) 8

Explanation of Sample Problem

The sample problem gives the student an equation that has one missing part. The student's job is to determine what number will correctly complete the mathematical sentence.

The answer to the sample problem is *B*. Since the problem presents an equation with a missing number, the students should determine which number correctly fills in the blank. The first step is multiplying 2 by 3, which yields 6. Then the student can determine what number can be subtracted from 10 to get 6. The answer for the missing number is 4. In order to check the answer and make sure that it is correct, the number can be substituted into the equation, and the equation can be simplified. 10 minus 4 yields 6 on the left side, while 2 times 3 yields 6 on the right side. This confirms that the problem has been worked out correctly.

Number Analogies

Description

In the Number Analogies section of the Level 9 CogAT test, the student's problem-solving ability will be tested as they reason through two given sets of numbers and apply the same operation to a third set that includes a missing number. The questions in this section will give students two sets of numbers that are complete, and they will have to determine what operation leads from the first number to the second number. They will then have to apply this operation to the third set in order to find the missing number.

Number Analogy questions require students to recognize what is happening to the first two sets of numbers before applying that operation to the third set. Sometimes the operations are simple addition and subtraction, and sometimes they require more complex work.

Relevance

Number analogies can be relevant for students as they recognize that there is a certain output value that corresponds to a certain input value. This will be helpful when they see functions in future math classes. Functions are used to model behavior and make predictions for what may happen to a given input value. Students begin the first steps of understanding functions as they recognize the "rules" that are applied to each of the first two groups of numbers and then follow that same "rule" to get the final answer for the third set of numbers.

Tips for Parents

The Number Analogies questions give students two sets of numbers and then ask them to fill in the third set. It is important for students to recognize what the question is asking of them in order to fill in the correct number.

First, students should notice the two sets of given numbers and use them to determine the operation used in both of them. The operation must be the same for both sets. Then they should apply that operation to the third set. This should yield the missing number. After filling in the missing number, the pattern will be the same for all three sets.

Sample Problem

The following problem is a sample of what students might see in the Number Analogies section of the test.

$$(2 \rightarrow 6) \quad (5 \rightarrow 9) \quad (8 \rightarrow ?)$$

a) 4   b) 12   c) 16   d) 20

Explanation of Sample Problem

The sample problem gives students three sets of numbers. The first two sets are complete, and there is a pattern as to how the second number was found in relation to the first. Students should figure out the pattern from the first two sets and apply it to the third set.

In this specific example, the pattern is adding four to the first number. Adding 4 to 2 gives the number 6. Adding 4 to 5 gives the number 9. In order to fill in the missing number, 4 is added to 8 to give the answer 12. The answer to the sample problem is *B*, 12.

Practice Questions

1.

3, 6, 9, 12, ___

a) 14   b) 18   c) 15   d) 21

2.

60, 30, 15, ___

a) 10   b) 7.5   c) 10.5   d) 7

3.

12 - 5 = 5 + ?

a) 2   b) 12   c) 7   d) 5

4.

3 × 2 = 10 - ?

a) 4   b) 6   c) 5   d) 3

5.

(4→16) (6→24) (8→?)

a) 12   b) 16   c) 40   d) 32

Answer Explanations

1. C: This series is counting by multiples of 3, or adding 3 each time. $12 + 3 = 15$.

2. B: The numbers in this series are being cut in half, or divided by 2. Half of 15 is 7.5.

3. A: The left side of the equation is equal to 7. To make the right side equal 7, 2 must be added to 5.

4. A: The left side of the equation equals 6. To make the right side equivalent, 10 must be subtracted by 4.

5. D: The first number in each set is multiplied by 4, and $8 \times 4 = 32$.

19

Nonverbal

Figure Matrices

Description

In the Figure Matrices section of the Level 10 CogAT test, the student's problem-solving ability will be tested as they reason through changing, visual aspects among diagrams. Each problem will contain a two-by-two grid with one blank space. The two top images will have a relationship that must be determined and applied to the bottom image to figure out which answer choice completes the grid.

This section is very similar to the Quantitative questions that ask to find the next number in the series. Because these questions involve diagrams, there is an extra layer of difficulty for students to reason through. Many times, more than one operation is applied to the given diagrams. It is important for students to pay attention to the different elements that may change, including position and shading.

Relevance

This section requires a great deal of "out of the box" thinking. One-dimensional thinking will not enable students to understand figure matrices; they must apply many concepts to the given problem. This ability to branch out using different ways of thinking can be very helpful in solving a variety of problems.

Tips for Parents

Spatial recognition is an important aspect in this section. Students must analyze the pictures and diagrams and see how they can be manipulated to find the answer that completes the matrix. Common changes include color and orientation of shapes that may change through rotation or reflection.

Students should practice for this section by viewing different matrices and determining how they are changed. As students work with more matrices, they will become familiar with the various patterns and be able to apply them to the given diagrams.

Sample Problem

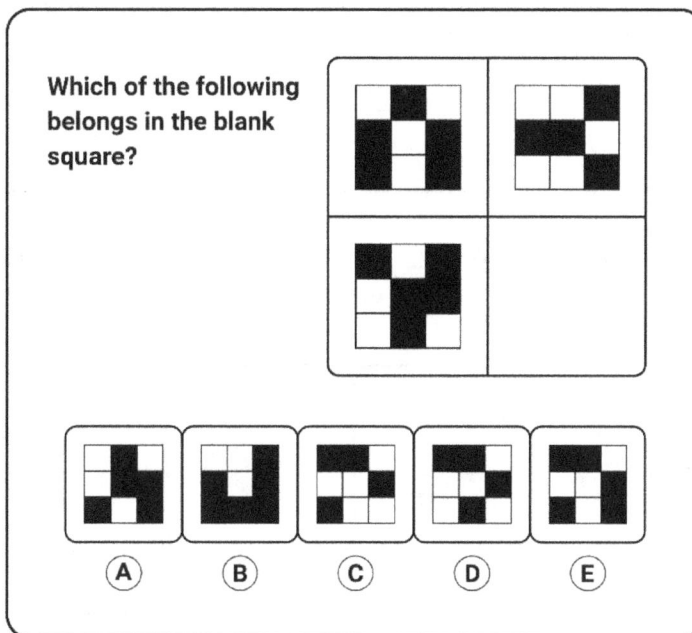

Explanation of Sample Problem

The answer is *C*. Looking at the relationship between the first two squares, two things changed. First, everything flipped to the right. Second, the coloring swapped (the black squares have become white, and the white squares have become black). To determine the answer, the bottom square must be flipped to the right and then its colors must be changed to their opposites. This leaves Choice *C* as the correct answer.

Paper Folding

Description

In the Paper Folding section of the Level 10 CogAT test, the student's analytical thinking will be tested. They will be asked to pick the diagram that shows how a folded, hole-punched piece of paper will look once it is unfolded. Students will have to evaluate where the holes are located, where the paper was folded, and how many times it was folded. Then they will have to determine where these holes will end up once the paper is unfolded.

Relevance

This section requires students to use logical reasoning to extrapolate a broader conclusion from a smaller amount of data. They will have to visualize how the changes made to the paper will affect it once unfolded. Students can use such critical thinking skills to visualize and determine the effects of an action.

Tips for Parents

A simple way for parents to prepare students for this section is to practice this hands-on activity. Start with a square piece of paper and have the student fold it in half twice. Then use a hole-punch to put

21

holes in the paper. Starting with a couple of holes will make it easier for the student to visualize where they end up once unfolded. Try to have the child predict where the holes will end up before the paper is unfolded. This strategy will get students thinking about spatial recognition and familiarize them with these types of diagrams so they can recognize them on the test.

Sample Problem

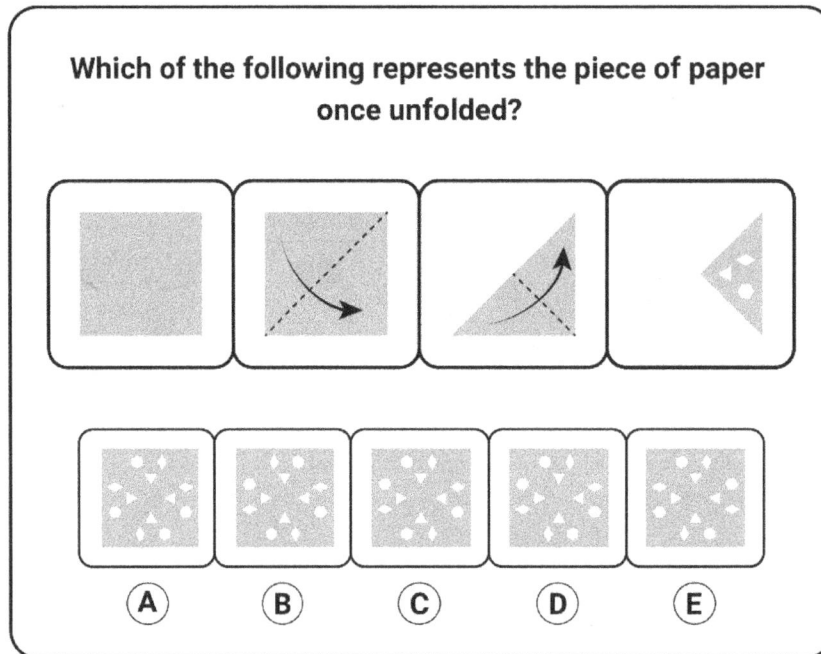

Explanation of Sample Problem

The answer is *D*. Choice *E* can be eliminated immediately because the correct original pattern is not present on the right side. Choices *B* and *C* should be ruled out because a circle will be on the right side at the bottom, since the paper will unfold down and to the left (the opposite of the way it was folded as indicated in the image). Lastly, since the paper folds diagonally across the square, the bottom half right should be a mirror image of the top half left. The only image that meets these criteria is Choice *D*, which is the correct answer.

Figure Classification

Description

In the Figure Classification section of the Level 10 CogAT test, the student's ability to recognize patterns and apply them to given situations will be tested. For each question, students will be presented with figures that are arranged or appear in a pattern. The pattern may be based on shape, size, color, etc. It

22

will be the student's job to recognize the pattern in the given diagrams and apply that same pattern to choose the next picture.

Relevance
The relevance of this section can be seen in many areas of life. In the real world, it is important to be able to recognize patterns, whether good or bad, and make smart choices based on those patterns. As a parent, seeing specific patterns in a child's life may lead to a certain action. If a child plays video games every day after school, and his grades begin to drop around the same time, then the parent may reevaluate the time that the student spends playing games.

Recognition of patterns can also motivate positive choices. If a child wants to get better at a certain sport, he may start practicing every day. If practice becomes a pattern, it will most likely result in better skill and a more positive outlook on the game. When students are better able to recognize patterns, they will also be better able to change the bad ones or continue the good ones.

Tips for Parents
To prepare students for this section, it may be helpful to use hands-on materials just as with paper folding. Prepare a set of materials that have something in common, present them to the student, and ask the student to describe which object would follow the last given item. Then talk with the student about the existing pattern and how the material they chose fits the pattern.

Another way to practice is by drawing a pattern of shapes or diagrams and then giving the student a few shapes to choose from as the answer. Once the student chooses the correct shape or diagram, the parent can ask why the other objects do not fit. Explaining the wrong choices can help deepen the student's understanding.

Sample Problem

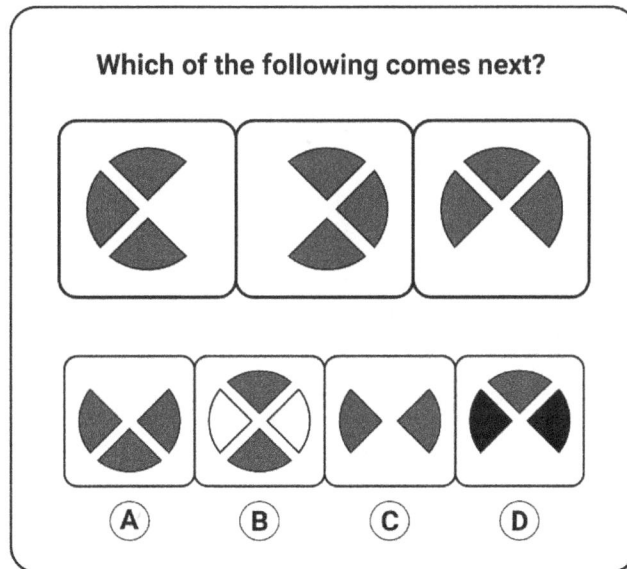

Which of the following comes next?

(A) (B) (C) (D)

Explanation of Sample Problem
The answer is *A*. Each image in the pattern depicts three pieces of a pie shaded in the same color. One has a missing piece on the right, the next has a missing piece on the left, and the last one has a missing

piece on the bottom. To complete the pattern, the missing piece needs to be on the top, which is shown in Choice *A*.

Practice Questions

1.

Which of the following belongs in the blank square?

Ⓐ Ⓑ Ⓒ Ⓓ Ⓔ

2.

Which of the following belongs in the blank square?

Ⓐ Ⓑ Ⓒ Ⓓ Ⓔ

3.

Which of the following represents the piece
of paper once unfolded?

Ⓐ   Ⓑ   Ⓒ   Ⓓ   Ⓔ

4.

Which of the following comes next?

Ⓐ   Ⓑ   Ⓒ   Ⓓ

5.

Which of the following comes next?

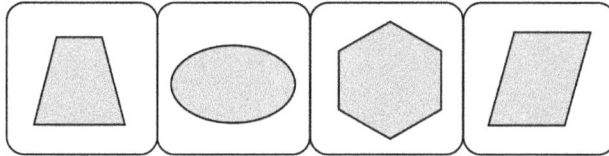

See answers on next page.

Answer Explanations

1. C

2. E

3. E

4. B

5. C

Verbal

Verbal Classification

1.

> # blue, red, yellow
> ___
> a) sun   b) green   c) top

2.

> # one, five, three
> ___
> a) cups   b) red   c) seven

3.

> # squash, broccoli, potato
> ___
> a) fruit   b) corn   c) vegetable

4.

basketball, baseball, football

---

a) time   b) sports   c) soccer

5.

tooth brush, toothpaste, floss

---

a) mouthwash   b) light   c) teeth

6.

shirt, shorts, belt

---

a) hat   b) sad   c) food

7.

sad, happy, glad

a) confused   b) water   c) car

8.

hamburger, hot dog, steak

a) meat   b) water   c) chicken

9.

sister, brother, mother

a) love   b) family   c) father

10.

lion, tiger, bear

a) animal   b) monkey   c) mammal

11.

pens, markers, pencils
_____
a) board   b) crayons   c) write

12.

Georgia, Florida, Arizona
_____
a) people   b) Texas   c) town

13.

bus, car, train
_____
a) bike   b) travel   c) happy

14.

fish, octopus, whale
---
a) dog   b) boat   c) shark

15.

grass, flowers, bushes
---
a) vegetables   b) weeds   c) outside

16.

golf, tennis, soccer
---
a) sports   b) basketball   c) exercise

17.

cow, chicken, goat

a) shark   b) animals   c) pig

18.

finger, knee, arm

a) shirt   b) leg   c) body part

19.

pentagon, octagon, triangle

a) hexagon   b) shape   c) color

20.

green, red, blue

a) shapes   b) rainbow   c) orange

Verbal Analogies

1.

apple: fruit - carrot:

a) vegetable   c) ground
b) orange   d) cucumber

2.

airplane: pilot - train:

a) cab   c) engineer
b) travel   d) tracks

3.

hand: finger - foot:

a) arm   c) shoe
b) toe   d) floor

4.

head: hat - hand:

a) finger   c) glove
b) toe   d) hat

5.

drink: cup - eat:

a) plate   c) order
b) food   d) pay

6.

bat: ball - bow:

a) arrow   c) ball
b) shoot   d) sport

7.

light: dark - wide:

a) short   c) narrow
b) tall   d) big

8.

bird: nest - dog:

a) puppy   c) house
b) kitten   d) coop

9.

lion: pride - wolf:

a) pack   c) pride

b) dog   d) gaggle

10.

school: fish - gaggle:

a) geese   c) birds

b) kittens   d) sun

11.

big: small - hot:

a) warm   c) boiling

b) cold   d) sun

12.

cow: calf - dog:

_____

a) cat   c) bed

b) puppy   d) lion

13.

early: late - happy:

_____

a) good   c) joyful

b) glowing   d) sad

14.

hint: clue - show:

_____

a) reveal   c) open

b) light   d) close

15.

winter: January - summer:

_____

a) calendar   c) July

b) month   d) February

16.

up: down - top:
_____

   a) bottom   c) up
   b) down   d) place

17.

grass: green - snow:
_____

   a) weather   c) white
   b) rain   d) color

18.

ear: hear - nose:
_____

   a) smell   c) small
   b) face   d) head

19.

pizza: cheese - burger:

a) eat   c) ketchup
b) food   d) top

20.

sing: song - read:

a) sit   c) talk
b) book   d) radio

21.

cloud: sky - lava:

a) red   c) hot
b) slow   d) volcano

22.

shop: store - play:

a) run   c) park
b) action d) exercise

23.

touch: hand - see:

a) eyes   c) glasses
b) hand   d) body part

24.

car: gas - fire:

a) water   c) rain
b) wood   d) tools

Sentence Completion

1.

He decided to wear his rainboots because it was _____ outside.

a) dry   b) hot   c) wet

2.

Mom was in a rush out the door because she was _____ for work.

a) late   b) early   c) sad

3.

The pot is hot, but the drink is _____.

a) cold   b) hot   c) big

4.

He decided to hang the shirt up because it was still _____.

a) angry   b) dry   c) wet

5.

> I could not buy the shirt with my money because it was too _____.
>
> _____
>
> a) sad   b) expensive   c) warm

6.

> Martin is _____than Shana because Martin was born before her.
>
> _____
>
> a) older   b) younger   c) happier

7.

> Joe brought his bat and ball to_____practice.
>
> _____
>
> a) dislike   b) baseball   c) love

8.

I had a bad haircut so I decided
to wear a _____.

a) shirt   b) hat   c) clothes

9.

During the soccer game, the players
listened to the _____.

a) coach   b) teacher   c) doctor

10.

The test caused Amy to be_____
because she was not prepared.

a) upset   b) happy   c) glad

11.

At the end of the football game, the team with the most points_____.
_____

a) loses   b) wins   c) jersey

12.

Anna was _____ because she did not finish her dinner.
_____

a) hungry   b) angry   c) tired

13.

The boy burned himself when he spilled the coffee because it was_____.
_____

a) drink   b) hot   c) cold

14.

> # The boy fell off the swing and_____ his arm.
>
> a) hurt   b) fixed   c) healed

15.

> # The clothes were _____, so Mom decided to wash them.
>
> a)clean   b) dirty   c) small

16.

> # Strawberries_____on the ground.
>
> a) grow   b) sunlight   c) water

17.

Joey wanted to _____ the TV because his favorite show was coming on.
_____

a) show   b) sit   c) watch

18.

He had to leave work _____ to make it to the baseball game.
_____

a) sad   b) late   c) early

19.

Steven wanted to ride in the _____ to the store.
_____

a) chair   b) car   c) bike

20.

> **The children had to stay inside and play because it was _____ outside.**
>
> a) dry   b) raining   c) warm

Quantitative

Number Series

1.

> # 3, 6, 12, 24, ____
>
> a) 30   b) 36   c) 48   d) 54

2.

> # 1, 2.5, 4, 5.5, ____
>
> a) 7   b) 9   c) 7.5   d) 11

3.

5, 10, 15, ____

a) 20   b) 24   c) 36   d) 54

4.

20, 10, 5, ____

a) 2   b) 2.5   c) 3   d) 1

5.

8, 15, 22, 29, ____

a) 20   b) 24   c) 36   d) 54

6.

6.5, 9, 11.5, 14, ___

a) 22   b) 17   c) 16.5   d) 15.5

7.

2, 4, 6, ___

a) 8   b) 12   c) 14   d) 10

8.

1, 2, 4, ___

a) 12   b) 10   c) 6   d) 8

9.

16, 12, 8, 4, ____

a) 5   b) 0   c) 2   d) 6

10.

2.5, 6.5, 9.5, ____

a) 20   b) 15   c) 12.5   d) 11.5

11.

1.75, 3, 4.25, 5.5, ____

a) 6.75   b) 8   c) 7.25   d) 9.5

12.

50, 60, 70, 80, ___

a) 20   b) 90   c) 100   d) 85

13.

7.2, 8.2, 9.2, 10.2, ___

a) 14.2   b) 12.2   c) 12   d) 11.2

14.

3.75, 2.5, 1.25, ___

a) 1   b) 0.25   c) 0.5   d) 0

15.

2, 3, 5, 6, ___

a) 4   b) 8   c) 7   d) 9

16.

2, 6, 10, 14, ___

a) 18   b) 20   c) 16   d) 24

17.

4, 5.75, 7.5, 9.25, ___

a) 12.25   b) 12   c) 11.5   d) 11

18.

$$0.75, 1.5, 3, 6, \underline{\quad}$$

a) 14   b) 12   c) 9   d) 16

Number Puzzles

1.

$$4 + (6 + ?) = 3 + (4 + 6)$$

a) 3   b) 10   c) 13   d) 6

2.

$$5 + (5 + ?) = 8 + (5 + 5)$$

a) 10   b) 5   c) 8   d) 23

3.

$$(6 + 2) + 7 = 2 + (? + 6)$$

a) 6   b) 11   c) 15   d) 7

4.

$$8 - ? = 3 + 2$$

a) 2   b) 3   c) 5   d) 6

5.

$$4 + 7 = 6 + ?$$

a) 6   b) 5   c) 7   d) 10

6.

$$8 + 6 - ? = 3 + 10$$

a) 2   b) 1   c) 14   d) 8

7.

$$10 - 3 = 5 + ?$$

a) 1   b) 7   c) 5   d) 2

8.

$$(2 + 3) + 7 = 3 + (2 + ?)$$

a) 7   b) 12   c) 14   d) 6

9.

$$1 + ? = 12 - 7$$

a) 8   b) 6   c) 5   d) 4

10.

$$8 - 6 = 1 + ?$$

a) 3   b) 4   c) 1   d) 2

11.

$$4 + (6 + 6) = (5 + 7) + ?$$

a) 4   b) 12   c) 8   d) 6

12.

$$4 - ? = 9 - 6$$

a) 0   b) 3   c) 1   d) 2

13.

$$4 + 11 = 3 \times ?$$

a) 5   b) 15   c) 10   d) 4

14.

$$4 \times 2 = 6 + ?$$

a) 6   b) 2   c) 8   d) 0

15.

$$? \times 3 = 1 + 5$$

a) 4   b) 1   c) 2   d) 6

16.

$$2 + 7 = 3 \times ?$$

a) 3   b) 1   c) 2   d) 4

Number Analogies

1.

$$(8 \rightarrow 64) \quad (5 \rightarrow 40) \quad (3 \rightarrow ?)$$

a) 9   b) 16   c) 21   d) 24

2.

$$(12 \rightarrow 24)\ (15 \rightarrow 30)\ (8 \rightarrow ?)$$

a) 24   b) 16   c) 20   d) 42

3.

$$(2 \rightarrow 3)\ (5 \rightarrow 6)\ (8 \rightarrow ?)$$

a) 7   b) 16   c) 10   d) 9

4.

$$(3 \rightarrow 9)\ (7 \rightarrow 21)\ (1 \rightarrow ?)$$

a) 3   b) 0   c) 7   d) 15

5.

$$(4 \rightarrow 16) \quad (8 \rightarrow 32) \quad (2 \rightarrow ?)$$

a) 10 b) 6 c) 8 d) 4

6.

$$(1 \rightarrow 0) \quad (5 \rightarrow 4) \quad (9 \rightarrow ?)$$

a) 8 b) 7 c) 6 d) 10

7.

$$(10 \rightarrow 6) \quad (25 \rightarrow 21) \quad (8 \rightarrow ?)$$

a) 12 b) 10 c) 6 d) 4

8.

$$(8 \rightarrow 9) \quad (4 \rightarrow 6) \quad (6 \rightarrow ?)$$

---

a) 12   b) 7   c) 8   d) 9

9.

$$(10 \rightarrow 7) \quad (14 \rightarrow 11) \quad (8 \rightarrow ?)$$

---

a) 11   b) 5   c) 4   d) 2

10.

$$(2 \rightarrow 12) \quad (5 \rightarrow 15) \quad (10 \rightarrow ?)$$

---

a) 25   b) 15   c) 18   d) 20

11.

$$(15 \rightarrow 23) \ (11 \rightarrow 19) \ (7 \rightarrow ?)$$

a) 13   b) 17   c) 21   d) 15

12.

$$(2 \rightarrow 9) \ (15 \rightarrow 22) \ (12 \rightarrow ?)$$

a) 18   b) 19   c) 20   d) 14

13.

$$(23 \rightarrow 10) \ (33 \rightarrow 20) \ (13 \rightarrow ?)$$

a) 0   b) 2   c) 3   d) 5

14.

$$(20 \rightarrow 10) \ (16 \rightarrow 8) \ (4 \rightarrow ?)$$

a) 1   b) 6   c) 2   d) 4

15.

$$(10 \rightarrow 30) \ (50 \rightarrow 70) \ (20 \rightarrow ?)$$

a) 30   b) 25   c) 35   d) 40

16.

$$(5 \rightarrow 15) \ (6 \rightarrow 18) \ (8 \rightarrow ?)$$

a) 32   b) 12   c) 16   d) 24

17.

$$(15 \rightarrow 11) \ (24 \rightarrow 20) \ (5 \rightarrow ?)$$

a) 5   b) 1   c) 0   d) 2

18.

$$(19 \rightarrow 12) \ (15 \rightarrow 8) \ (8 \rightarrow ?)$$

a) 1   b) 3   c) 5   d) 4

Nonverbal

Figure Matrices

1.

Which of the following belongs in the blank square?

A   B   C   D   E

2.

Which of the following belongs in the blank square?

A   B   C   D   E

3.

Which of the following belongs in the blank square?

A B C D E

4.

Which of the following belongs in the blank square?

A   B   C   D   E

5.

Which of the following belongs in the blank square?

A   B   C   D   E

6.

Which of the following belongs in the blank square?

A   B   C   D   E

7.

Which of the following belongs in the blank square?

A   B   C   D   E

8.

Which of the following belongs in the blank square?

A B C D E

9.

Which of the following belongs in the blank square?

A   B   C   D   E

10.

Which of the following belongs in the blank square?

A   B   C   D   E

11.

Which of the following belongs in the blank square?

A   B   C   D   E

12.

Which of the following belongs in the blank square?

A   B   C   D   E

13.

Which of the following belongs in the blank square?

14.

Which of the following belongs in the blank square?

A   B   C   D   E

15.

Which of the following belongs in the blank square?

16.

Which of the following belongs in the blank square?

(A) (B) (C) (D) (E)

17.

Which of the following belongs in the blank square?

A   B   C   D   E

18.

Which of the following belongs in the blank square?

A B C D E

19.

Which of the following belongs in the blank square?

A   B   C   D   E

20.

Which of the following belongs in the blank square?

A   B   C   D   E

Paper Folding

1.

Which of the following represents the piece of paper once unfolded?

(A)   (B)   (C)   (D)   (E)

2.

Which of the following represents the piece of paper once unfolded?

A   B   C   D   E

3.

Which of the following represents the piece of paper once unfolded?

A   B   C   D   E

4.

Which of the following represents the piece of paper once unfolded?

(A) (B) (C) (D) (E)

5.

Which of the following represents the piece of paper once unfolded?

(A) (B) (C) (D) (E)

6.

Which of the following represents the piece of paper once unfolded?

A   B   C   D   E

7.

Which of the following represents the piece of paper once unfolded?

A   B   C   D   E

8.

Which of the following represents the piece of paper once unfolded?

9.

Which of the following represents the piece of paper once unfolded?

A   B   C   D   E

10.

Which of the following represents the piece of paper once unfolded?

Ⓐ   Ⓑ   Ⓒ   Ⓓ   Ⓔ

11.

Which of the following represents the piece of paper once unfolded?

12.

Which of the following represents the piece of paper once unfolded?

13.

Which of the following represents the piece of paper once unfolded?

(A) (B) (C) (D) (E)

14.

Which of the following represents the piece of paper once unfolded?

A   B   C   D   E

15.

Which of the following represents the piece of paper once unfolded?

A B C D E

16.

Which of the following represents the piece of paper once unfolded?

Figure Classification

1.

Which of the following comes next?

A   B   C   D

2.

Which of the following comes next?

3.

Which of the following comes next?

(A) (B) (C) (D)

4.

Which of the following comes next?

A B C D

5.

Which of the following comes next?

6.

Which of the following comes next?

A   B   C   D

7.

Which of the following comes next?

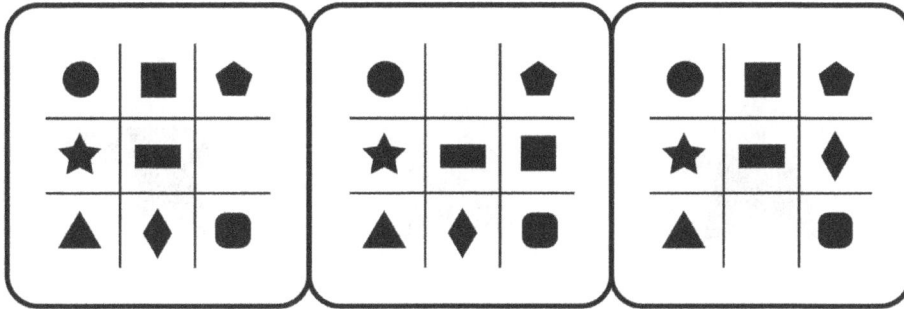

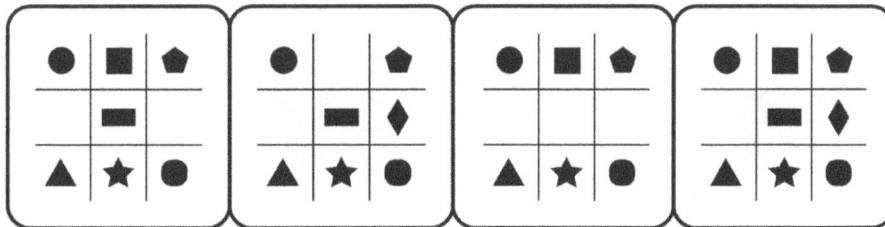

8.

Which of the following comes next?

9.

Which of the following comes next?

A   B   C   D

10.

Which of the following comes next?

11.

Which of the following comes next?

A   B   C   D

12.

Which of the following comes next?

A   B   C   D

13.

Which of the following comes next?

A   B   C   D

14.

Which of the following comes next?

A   B   C   D

15.

Which of the following comes next?

A   B   C   D

16.

Which of the following comes next?

A   B   C   D

17.

Which of the following comes next?

A   B   C   D

18.

Which of the following comes next?

A B C D

19.

Which of the following comes next?

20.

Which of the following comes next?

Answer Explanations

Verbal

Verbal Classification

1. B: The given words are colors. The only color in the answer choices is green.

2. C: The given words are numbers. Choice *C, seven,* is in the same category.

3. B: The given words are vegetables. The vegetable from the choices is *corn.* While *vegetable* is an answer choice, it is not the correct answer because it describes the group and is not itself a type of vegetable.

4. C: The given words are different sports. The answer choice that fits this classification is *soccer.* While *sports* is an answer choice, it describes the overall classification but does not fit into the group.

5. A: The given words are tools used to clean teeth. *Mouthwash* is part of this group. *Teeth* are not a tool in the process of cleaning teeth, so that cannot be the correct answer.

6. A: The given words describe things that people wear. Choice *A,* hat, is also an article of clothing.

7. A: The given words describe emotions. *Confused* is another example of an emotion.

8. C: The given words are meats that people eat. *Chicken* is another type of meat that people can eat. While *meat* is an option, it is not the correct choice because it describes the classification.

9. C: The words in the given group are family members. *Father* is the only family member listed as an answer choice.

10. B: The given words are animals. The only animal in the answer choices is *monkey.*

11. B: The given words describe writing utensils. *Crayons* are another type of writing utensil.

12. B: The words in the given group can be classified as states. Texas is a state in the United States.

13. A: The given words describe different means of travel. A *bike* is another means of travel.

14. C: The given words are ocean animals. A *shark* is also an ocean animal.

15. B: The given words describe things that grow outside or in the yard. *Weeds* grow in the yard. While *vegetables* grow outside, they more often grow in a garden than in a yard.

16. B: The given words are sports. *Basketball* is the only sport listed as an answer choice.

17. C: The given words are farm animals. A *pig* is a farm animal.

18. B: The given words can be classified as body parts, and a *leg* is part of the body.

19. A: The words in the given group can be classified as shapes, or more specifically polygons. A *hexagon* is a six-sided polygon.

20. C: The given words are colors. *Orange* is the correct answer because it too is a color. *Rainbow* is a related word, but it describes many colors, while all of the given words name individual colors.

Verbal Analogies

1. A: An apple is classified as a fruit, while a carrot is classified as a vegetable.

2. C: An airplane is driven by a pilot, while a train is driven by an engineer.

3. B: A finger is found on a hand, while a toe is found on a foot.

4. C: A hat is worn on the head, while a glove is worn on the hand.

5. A: A cup is used to drink from, while a plate is used to eat from.

6. A: A bat is used to hit a ball, while a bow is used to shoot an arrow.

7. C: Light is the opposite of dark, while wide is the opposite of narrow.

8. C: A bird lives in a nest, while a dog lives in a house.

9. A: A lion travels in a group called a pride, while a wolf travels in a group called a pack.

10. A: Fish travel in a group called a school, while geese travel in a group called a gaggle.

11. B: Big is the opposite of small, while hot is the opposite of cold.

12. B: A mother cow has a baby called a calf, while a mother dog has a baby called a puppy.

13. D: Early is the opposite of late, while happy is the opposite of sad.

14. A: Hint and clue are synonyms, just as show and reveal.

15. C: January is a month in the season of winter, while July is a month during the season of summer.

16. A: Up is the opposite of down, while top is the opposite of bottom.

17. C: Grass is green, while snow is white.

18. A: The ear is used for hearing, while the nose is used for smelling.

19. C: Cheese can be a topping that is put on pizza, while ketchup can be a topping that is put on a burger.

20. B: A song is meant to be sung, while a book is meant to be read.

124

21. D: Clouds are found in the sky, while lava is found in a volcano.

22. C: A store is where people go to shop, while a park is where people go to play.

23. A: The hand is the body part that touches, while the eyes are the body parts that see.

24. B: Gas fuels a car, and wood fuels a fire.

Sentence Completion

1. C: The boy wore his rainboots because it was wet outside.

2. A: Mom was in a rush because she was late.

3. A: The pot is hot, but the drink is cold. The transition word "but" means the condition of the pot will be the opposite of the drink.

4. C: The shirt was still wet, so it needed to be hung up.

5. B: The shirt could not be bought because it was too expensive, or it cost too much.

6. A: Martin was born before Shana, so he is older than her.

7. B: Baseball practice is a place where Joe would need to bring his bat and ball.

8. B: Wearing a hat would cover up the bad haircut.

9. A: During a game, the players should listen to their coach for instruction.

10. A: Since Amy was not prepared for the test, she was upset.

11. B: At the end of a football game, the winner is determined by which team has earned the most points.

12. A: Since Anna did not finish her dinner, she got hungry.

13. B: The boy was burned because the coffee was hot when he spilled it on himself.

14. A: The boy hurt his arm when he fell off the swing.

15. B: When clothes are dirty, they need to be washed.

16. A: Strawberries are found growing on the ground in the right season.

17. C: If Joey wanted to see his favorite show, he would need to watch the TV.

18. C: For him to make it to the game, he needed to leave work early to give himself extra time.

19. B: A car is something people ride in when they need to travel to the store. While Steven could potentially ride a bike to the store, he would ride *on* a bike, not *in* it.

20. B: The rain outside prevented the children from playing outside; instead, they had to stay inside to keep dry.

Quantitative

Number Series

1. C: The correct answer is *C* because the pattern is multiplying by two. Multiplying 24 by 2 results in the answer of 48.

2. A: In this series, each number increases by 1.5. Adding 1.5 to 5.5 results in 7.

3. A: The series shows numbers that increase by five each time. Counting by 5 gives the numbers 5, 10, 15, and 20.

4. B: The series in this problem is found by taking half of each number. Half of 5 is 2.5.

5. C: Each number in this series is found by adding 7 to the previous number. $29 + 7 = 36$.

6. C: The numbers in this series are found by adding 2.5 to each consecutive number. $14 + 2.5 = 16.5$.

7. A: This is a set even numbers that increase by 2 each time. The even number that comes after 4 is 6.

8. D: The numbers in this set are doubled each time. 1 doubled becomes 2, which doubles to 4, which doubles to 8.

9. B: Each number in the series is reduced by 4. When 4 is reduced by itself, the result is 0.

10. D: This series is more complex because the number being added each time decreases by one. Between the first two numbers, the increase is 4, then they increase by 3, and then by 2. $9.5 + 2 = 11.5$.

11. A: Each number in this series increases by 1.25. $5.5 + 1.25 = 6.75$.

12. B: These numbers are skip-counting, or increasing, by ten. 80 increased by 10 is 90.

13. D: The numbers in this series increase by one. $10.2 + 1 = 11.2$.

14. D: This series shows numbers that are decreasing by 1.25. Decreasing the last number by 1.25 results in 0.

15. B: The pattern of this series is adding 1, then adding 2, then adding 1, then adding 2. The last number needs to be increased by 2, resulting in 8.

16. A: Each number is increased by 4 to get the next number. $14 + 4 = 18$.

17. D: In this series of numbers, 1.75 is added to each number. $9.25 + 1.75 = 11$.

18. B: These numbers are doubled, or multiplied by 2. When 6 is doubled, the result is 12.

Number Puzzles

1. A: 3 is the only number that can make the number sentence true. This makes both sides of the equation equal to 13.

2. C: The equation on the right side adds up to 18. In order for the left side to be equal, the missing number must be 8.

3. D: The missing number is 7 because it is the number that makes both sides of the equation equal to 14.

4. B: This equation is different, but it requires the same type of thinking. The right side has a sum of 5, so the left side must have a difference of 5: $8 - 3 = 5$.

5. B: In order for this to be a true statement, the missing number must be 5. Both sides yield a sum of 11.

6. B: The total for the right side of the equation is 13. By adding 8 and 6 on the left side, the sum is 14. The difference between 13 and 14 is 1.

7. D: The mathematical statement must have a value of 7, and $5 + 2 = 7$.

8. A: The left side of the equation adds up to 12. The missing number must be 7 because makes the right side equal to 12 as well.

9. D: The difference of the right side is 5, so the sum on the left must be 5 also. 4 added to 1 yields 5.

10. C: $8 - 6 = 2$, so the right side must also equal 2. This can be achieved by adding 1 to 1.

11. A: The total on the left side is 16, so the number missing on the right side is 4.

12. C: The difference on the right side of the equation gives a value of 3. The number one can be subtracted from 4 to get an answer of three also.

13. A: The left side gives a sum of 15. The missing number must be 5 because the product of 3 and 5 is 15.

14. B: The product of 4 and 2 is 8. To make the right side equal, 2 must be added to 6.

15. C: The sum of the right side is 6. Factoring 6 results in 3 and 2, so the missing number is 2.

16. A: The sum of the left side is 9. The factors of 9 are 3, 9, and 1. Multiplying 3 by 3 yields a value of 9.

Number Analogies

1. D: Each set of numbers is multiplied by 8. Multiplying 3 by 8 results in 24.

2. B: The first number in each set is doubled. Multiplying 8 by 2 yields a missing number of 16.

3. D: These analogies are found by adding 1 to the given number: $8 + 1 = 9$.

4. A: The first number in each set is multiplied by 3, and $1 \times 3 = 3$.

5. C: The number analogy in this problem is multiplying by 4: $2 \times 4 = 8$.

6. A: The relationship between each set of numbers is a difference of 1. By subtracting 1 from 9, the answer is 8.

7. D: Each number is subtracted by 4, and $8 - 4 = 4$.

8. D: The number being added to the first item of each set increases by 1 each time:

$$8 + 1 = 9$$

$$4 + 2 = 6$$

$$6 + 3 = 9$$

9. B: The first number in each set decreased by 3: $8 - 3 = 5$.

10. D: In this set, 10 is added to the first number. When 10 is added to 10, the sum is 20.

11. D: The first number in each set is increased by 8. Adding 8 to 7 yields 15.

12. B: 7 is added to the first number, so $12 + 7 = 19$.

13. A: The difference between the numbers in the first two sets is 13. Using this pattern, the final number is 0 because $13 - 13 = 0$.

14. C: Each set of numbers is determined by taking half of the first number, and half of 4 is 2.

15. D: The first number of each set is increased by 20. When 20 is increased by 20, the result is 40.

16. D: In each set, the first number is multiplied by 3. In the last set, 8 is multiplied by 3 to get a total of 24.

17. B: Each set of numbers has a difference of 4, and $5 - 4 = 1$.

18. A: Each set has a difference of 7. When 8 is subtracted by 7, the result is 1.

Nonverbal

Figure Matrices

1. D

2. B

3. E

4. C

5. D

6. C

7. A

8. E

9. B

10. E

11. B

12. A

13. E

14. D

15. A

16. B

17. E

18. C

19. D

20. E

Paper Folding

1. E

2. B

3. D

4. C

5. E

6. A

7. A

8. B

9. C

10. E

Test Prep Books

11. D

12. C

13. B

14. A

15. E

16. C

Figure Classification

1. A

2. B

3. D

4. A

5. B

6. C

7. D

8. C

9. D

10. B

11. A

12. C

13. D

14. A

15. B

16. B

17. C

18. A

19. D

20. B

Dear Parent or Teacher,

Thank you again for purchasing this study guide for your child or student. We hope that we exceeded your expectations.

Our goal in creating this study guide was to introduce the student to the types of questions that will be found on their test. We also strove to make our practice questions as similar as possible to what the student will encounter on test day. With that being said, if you found something that you feel was not up to your standards, please send us an email and let us know.

We have study guides in a wide variety of fields. If you're interested in one for yourself or another one for your child, try searching for it on Amazon or send us an email.

Thanks Again and Happy Testing!
Product Development Team
info@studyguideteam.com

FREE Test Taking Tips Video/DVD Offer

To better serve you, we created videos covering test taking tips that we want to give you for FREE. **These videos cover world-class tips that will help you succeed on your test.**

We just ask that you send us feedback about this product. Please let us know what you thought about it—whether good, bad, or indifferent.

To get your **FREE videos**, you can use the QR code below or email freevideos@studyguideteam.com with "Free Videos" in the subject line and the following information in the body of the email:

  a. The title of your product

  b. Your product rating on a scale of 1-5, with 5 being the highest

  c. Your feedback about the product

If you have any questions or concerns, please don't hesitate to contact us at info@studyguideteam.com.

Thank you!

www.ingramcontent.com/pod-product-compliance
Lightning Source LLC
Chambersburg PA
CBHW081330090426

42737CB00017B/3081